curious about

DETECTION DOGS

BY CARI MEISTER

AMICUS LEARNING

What are you

curious about?

Curious About is published by
Amicus Learning, an imprint of Amicus
P.O. Box 227, Mankato, MN 56002
www.amicuspublishing.us

Editor: Ana Brauer
Series Designer: Kathleen Petelinsek
Book Designer and Photo Researcher: Sara Hood

Library of Congress Cataloging-in-Publication Data

Names: Meister, Cari author
Title: Curious about detection dogs / Cari Meister.
Description: Mankato, MN : Amicus Learning, [2026] | Series: Curious about working dogs | Includes bibliographical references and index. | Audience: Ages 6–9 | Audience: Grades 2–3 | Summary: "How good is a detection dog's nose? Learn about these incredible canines in this question-and-answer book for elementary-aged readers. Includes infographics, table of contents, glossary, books and websites for further research, and index"— Provided by publisher.
Identifiers: LCCN 2025012831 (print) | LCCN 2025012832 (ebook) | ISBN 9798892008532 library binding | ISBN 9798892009195 paperback | ISBN 9798892009850 ebook
Subjects: LCSH: Detector dogs—Juvenile literature | Detector dogs—Training—Juvenile literature | Detector dogs—Sense organs—Juvenile literature
Classification: LCC SF428.73 .M45 2026 (print) | LCC SF428.73 (ebook) | DDC 636.7/0886—dc23/eng/20250814
LC record available at https://lccn.loc.gov/2025012831
LC ebook record available at https://lccn.loc.gov/2025012832

Photo Credits: Alamy Stock Photo/GROSSEMY VANESSA, 6; DVIDS/Lance Cpl. Zachery B. Martin, cover, 1; Getty Images/ Bread and Butter Productions, 7, Catherine Falls Commercial, 20, Digital Vision., 21, Eleganza, 11, Fertnig, 18–19, Heather Paul, 5, LittleCityLifestylePhotography, 17, Lorado, 3, 16, Marco Vacca, 2, 12–13, Sebastian Gollnow/picture alliance, 2, 8–9, YANN SCHREIBER, 14; Shutterstock/Eric Isselee, 15 (middle), FabrikaSimf, 15 (top), Natalia Fedosova, 15 (second from top), otsphoto, 15 (bottom), Svetography, 15 (second from bottom); The Noun Project/April Yang, 22, 23, Icon Market, 22, 23

Printed in United States of America

CHAPTER ONE

What is a detection dog?

Detection dogs are super sniffers! These dogs use their noses to find things humans can't see. Dogs can smell drugs, bombs, and even lost people. Some dogs even find bed bugs or **mold** in houses!

WHAT CAN A DETECTION DOG SMELL?

bed bugs

bombs

drugs

mold

people

Detection dogs smell clothes to look for missing people or solve crimes.

Detection dogs are also called sniffer dogs.

How good is a detection dog's nose?

A dog's sense of smell is much better than yours. You have about 6 million smell **cells** in your nose. A dog has up to 300 million! They can smell tiny bits of things we can't. They can even smell through walls and under the ground!

A detection dog can find things buried up to 40 feet (12.2 meters) underground.

How do detection dogs help us?

They help keep people safe. At airports, they sniff bags for dangerous items. When someone gets lost in the woods, they use their amazing noses to follow that person's scent trail. They can even find people trapped in places.

Detection dogs at airports sniff bags to find things that shouldn't be there.

CHAPTER TWO

How do detection dogs know what to do?

They **train** at special places! Training starts like a fun game. Dogs learn to find a special toy that has the smell they need to detect. When the dogs find it, they get treats and praise. Soon, they learn to sit or lie down when they smell what they are looking for.

Detection dogs are given treats when they find something.

How long does it take to train a detection dog?

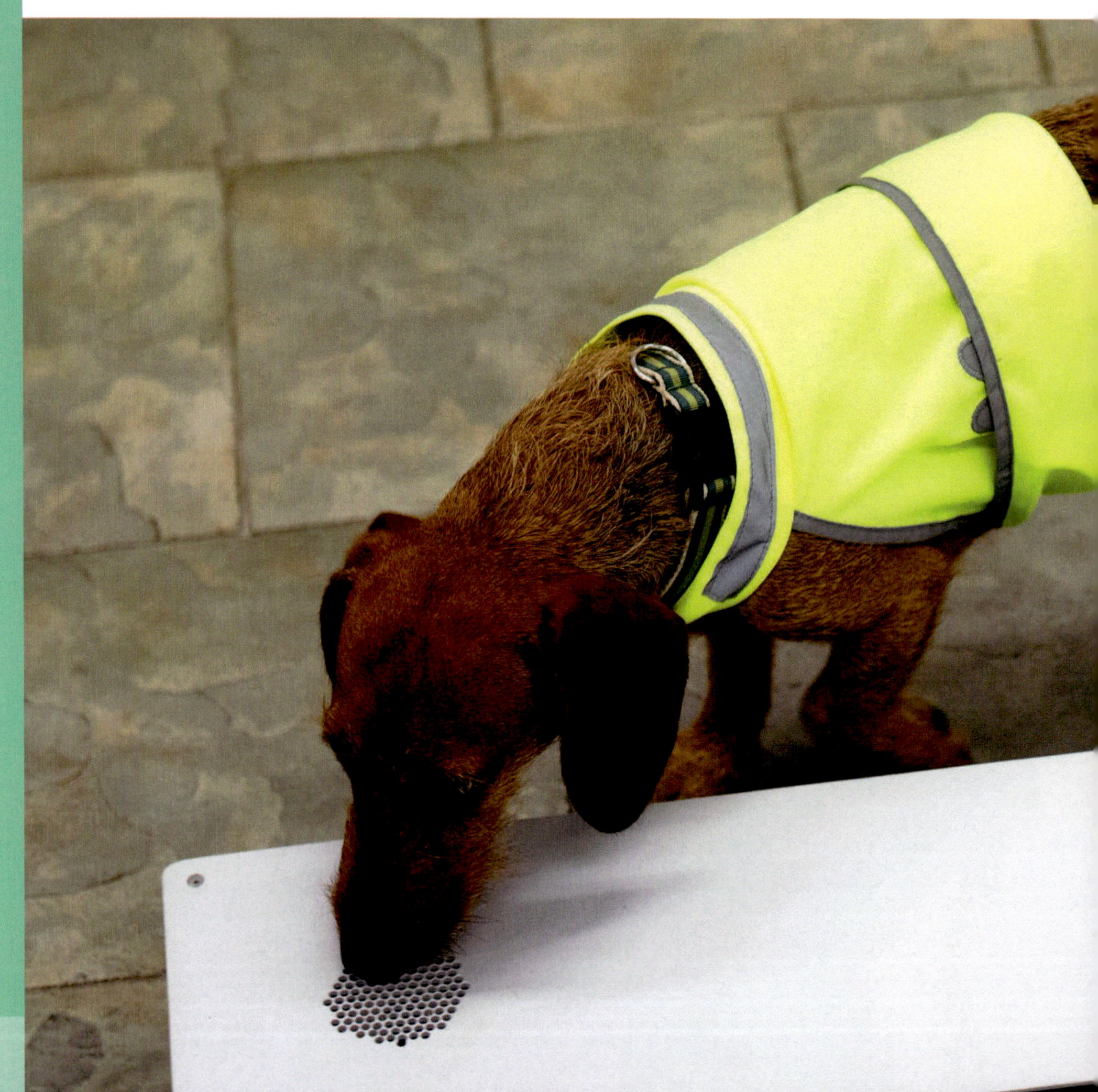

Most detection dogs train for about six months before they start working. They start learning when they are puppies. They practice every day. They search in different kinds of places. They learn to obey.

Most detection dogs start training at 10 months old.

DID YOU KNOW?
About 1 in 3 detection dogs that start training become working dogs.

Can any dog become a detection dog?

Golden retrievers make good detection dogs.

The best **breeds** for this kind of work are usually German Shepherds, Labrador Retrievers, and Belgian Malinois. These dogs love to work! They have great noses. Detection dogs must also be brave and calm in busy places.

GERMAN SHEPHERD

LABRADOR RETRIEVER

BELGIAN MALINOIS

BEAGLE

SPRINGER SPANIEL

Where do detection dogs live?

After work, detection dogs enjoy walks with their owners.

They live with their **handlers**. Their handlers feed them, play with them, and take them to the vet. At home, detection dogs are just like pets. They love to play and get belly rubs!

Off-duty detection dogs also love playtime.

What happens when a detection dog finds something?

They tell their handler in a special way. Some dogs sit down or lie down where the object is. Others bark or scratch. Their handler gives them praise and a treat as a reward.

Many police dogs work as detection dogs.

DID YOU KNOW?
One detection dog can search a room faster than three human police officers.

Do detection dogs ever mess up?

Dogs can get distracted, so their handlers help them stay focused.

Yes. Even the best dogs can make mistakes! Just like people, dogs can get tired, hungry, or distracted. When they make a mistake, they just try again. Handlers help keep their dogs alert by giving them breaks and treats.

DID YOU KNOW?
A detection dog takes a break every 30 minutes. This helps it stay focused.

Sometimes, detection dogs might think they smell something when there is nothing there.

ASK MORE QUESTIONS

How does a dog's nose work to detect smells?

How do detection dogs help find people after hurricanes?

Try a BIG QUESTION: How do detection dogs make our world safer?

SEARCH FOR ANSWERS

Search the library catalog or the Internet.
A librarian, teacher, or parent can help you.

Using Keywords
Find the looking glass.

Keywords are the most important words in your question.

?

If you want to know about:

- dog noses and smell, type: DOG SENSE OF SMELL
- how dogs help find people after hurricanes, type: DETECTION DOGS HURRICANES

FIND GOOD SOURCES

Here are some good, safe sources you can use in your research.
Your librarian can help you find more.

Books

Jobs of a Working Dog: Detection Dog
by B. Keith Davidson, 2022.

K-9 Police Dogs
by Cari Meister, 2026.

Internet Sites

American Working Dog
https://www.americanworkingdog.com/
This site gives information about types of working dogs and how to get involved.

FBI: About Our Dogs
https://archives.fbi.gov/archives/fun-games/kids/about-our-dogs-text-version
This site provides information about different kinds of working dogs.

Every effort has been made to ensure that these websites are appropriate for children. However, because of the nature of the Internet, it is impossible to guarantee that these sites will remain active indefinitely or that their contents will not be altered.

SHARE AND TAKE ACTION

Watch detection dogs work at a public demonstration at your local police department.

Make a poster about different types of detection dogs to share with your friends.

Practice nose work games with your dog using treats and toys.

GLOSSARY

breed A certain type of animal or plant.

cell One of the tiny units that are the basic building blocks of living things.

handler A person who works with and takes care of a detection dog.

mold A growth of fungus on damp or decaying material.

train To learn and practice special skills.

INDEX

About the Author

Cari Meister has written many books for children about dogs. She recently rescued a Great Dane puppy from an animal shelter. Cari loves learning about how dogs help keep communities safe. She lives in Vail, Colorado, and sees avalanche dogs at work all winter long.